YOUR KID I
DON'T SCREW HIM UP

MW00878039

Advice From

Stanley Stein, MD

A Pediatrician Practicing
For 55 Years

Copyright March 14, 2018

By **Stanley Stein, MD**

ISBN 10:1985384604

ISBN 13:9781985384606

The recommendations expressed in this book are solely the opinions of this author. Every child is different. If there are any questions about your baby, please consult a physician.

Contents

A page to page guide to your questions

Acknowledgments

I dedicate this book to Dr. Jerry Lucey. He was one of my medical school professors at University of Vermont, and if it were not for him, I would not have gone into pediatrics. He was an incredible, brilliant doctor who brought photo therapy for jaundiced babies to the United States.

I also want to dedicate this book to all of my patients, many of whom are fourth generation families. Thank you for the honor and joy of practicing pediatrics for 55 years.

Lastly, this book is dedicated to my wonderful wife of 58 years, my four daughters and son-in-laws, my 14 grandchildren and my great-grandson.

-Stan Stein, MD

A Child Lives

The Life He Learns

- If you are calm during pregnancy and as a parent, chances are your child will be as well.
- If you give your baby a pacifier, he will not learn to pacify himself.
- If you rock your baby every time he cries, he will not learn to soothe himself.
- If you keep the baby on your schedule from the beginning, he will adjust to your schedule.
- If you put a baby to bed when it is not perfectly silent, he will get used to going to sleep with surrounding noise.
- If you have fun with your child, he will likely have fun as well.
- If you are able to spend quality time with your child, you will be well on your way to building a beautiful family.

CHAPTER 1

PRENATAL

When should I start taking prenatal vitamins?

Three months prior to conceiving, the mother should begin taking prenatal vitamins with folic acid. At this time, you should also avoid any alcohol, tobacco and medications unless specifically prescribed by a physician with knowledge of your intention to become pregnant.

Haley Zimring, my granddaughter, pregnant with my first great-grandchild

When the mother is pregnant, anything she ingests will be passed on to her baby, which may have side effects. While acetaminophen (such as Tylenol) may be safe to take in certain instances, aspirin and ibuprofen (such as Advil) are not recommended during pregnancy.

How long is a full term pregnancy?

A full term pregnancy is usually referred to as nine months; however, it is actually 283 days or an average of 40 weeks. The time period is calculated from the first day of the mother's last menstrual cycle. We would consider anywhere from 37 to 42 weeks to be a full term pregnancy.

CHAPTER 2

HOSPITAL STAY

What tests/vaccines or other procedures are done in the hospital?

The physician along with the nurse will give babies an "Apgar" score based on five criteria, each worth two points. Therefore, a perfect score would be a ten with anything from a seven or above being satisfactory.

The five criteria are:

COLOR

- 0 - The whole body is blue which indicates lack of oxygen called cyanosis.
- 1 – The infant's hands and feet are blue while the rest of the body is a good color.

- 2 – The newborn's entire body is a good color.

RESPIRATORY RATE

- 0 – The newborn is not breathing and has no cry.
- 1 – The breathing is slow or irregular and the newborn has a weak cry.
- 2 – The breathing is normal and the baby has a good cry.

HEART RATE

- 0 - The newborn has no pulse.
- 1 – The baby's pulse is slow (under 100 beats per minute).
- 2 – The infant's pulse is normal (over 100 beats per minute).

ACTIVITY

- 0 - The newborn is limp.
- 1 – The child has little movement.
- 2 - The newborn is active.

REFLEXES

- 0 – The infant has no response when stimulated.

- 1 – The newborn has little response when stimulated.
- 2 – The baby responds when stimulated.

The Apgar test is performed at one minute and again at five minutes after birth. It is not uncommon for the first score to be low as a result of the stress of the delivery. This is why it is done again at five minutes to see if the newborn has recovered from the stress. If the newborn's score is less than seven, he will be put into the Neonatal Intensive Care Unit ("NICU") to be monitored.

The "Moro reflex" test is done to assess the baby's reflexes. By lightly startling the infant, the test is intended to trigger a reflexive reaction.

The infant is then given antibiotic eye drops, which are required in most states. These drops are to prevent sexually transmitted diseases, such as gonorrhea, that can be transmitted from the mother.

After these preliminary tests are performed we will check the baby's other vital signs and perform additional assessments. Within the first two days of the infant's life, a screening test is done to rule out many serious diseases including cystic fibrosis, sickle cell anemia, phenylketonuria

("PKU"), and other disorders which are quite uncommon but important to diagnose early. An early diagnosis may allow for treatments to manage and even prevent the serious consequences of some of these conditions which may include seizures, mental disability, and intellectual challenges. The newborn is also given a hearing test.

In the hospital, the infant will receive a shot of hepatitis B. This is the first of three shots your baby will receive for hepatitis B. The newborn is also given a shot of vitamin K to prevent bleeding.

Will the newborn stay in my room?

Most mothers prefer to have the infant with them constantly which is called "rooming in". Some newborns, however, will be kept in the nursery at the request of the mother. The mother may have several children at home and prefer to have a little rest in the hospital by having the nurses take care of the newborn and have the infant just brought in for feedings and visits.

How long is the hospital stay?

Most babies born by vaginal delivery stay in the hospital for 48 hours. Babies born by a Caesarean section usually stay for 72 hours.

Will my baby gain weight while in the hospital?

While in the hospital, the newborn will generally lose weight. By day six, the baby should start to gain weight back and by day ten, the infant should be back to his birth weight.

What is a circumcision?

A circumcision is the removal of the foreskin from the penis. A large percentage of babies born in the United States are circumcised.

Reasons for circumcisions:

- If the baby is not circumcised, the foreskin has to constantly be retracted (pulled back) so he

doesn't develop adhesions, which is extremely painful.
- Lowered risk of an infection of the penis.
- Lowered risk of cancer of the penis.

A circumcision is usually done in the hospital on the first or second day of life. Some religions are against a baby being circumcised. In the Jewish religion, they observe a ritual where a baby is circumcised by a physician or specially trained religious clergy on the eighth day of life. This procedure, called a bris, is done outside of a hospital.

How should I take care of the newborn after the circumcision?

After the circumcision leave the gauze on for 24 hours. Apply Vaseline for about 5 days with each diaper change. Contact your doctor if there is excessive bleeding, fever, redness or puss coming from the incision or if your newborn has trouble urinating. It will take about 10 to 14 days for the circumcised penis to completely heal.

How should I care for my infant's umbilical cord?

The caregiver should sponge bathe the infant avoiding the umbilical cord and surrounding area. Your goal is to keep this area dry and clean. Try to fold down the diaper underneath the belly button so it does not interfere with the umbilical cord and have the baby wear loose clothing. It should take approximately two weeks for the cord to fall off. After the umbilical cord falls off, you can then bathe your baby in an infant tub.

CHAPTER 3

PREMATURE BABIES

When is a baby premature?

A newborn that weighs less than approximately five and one-half pounds is considered premature. This weight is often achieved by the 37th week of pregnancy.

Many women who have gestational diabetes or other medical conditions will elect to have a cesarean section between 37 - 39 weeks of pregnancy.

With medical advances and competent neonatal teams, the infant may now survive if he is born as early as 25 weeks, although the newborn may only weigh about one and one-half pounds at birth.

If my newborn is premature, what should I expect?

The smaller the infant, the more likely there are to be complications and the longer the newborn will have to stay in the NICU. A premature baby is prone to have slower development and is more likely to have certain diseases depending primarily on his birth weight and gestational period.

CHAPTER 4

LIFE WITH A CHILD

Should my child be on a schedule?

Once a baby is born it is important to try to keep him on your schedule. Do not change your schedule to conform to the baby's schedule. I have no problem allowing the baby to go out with his parents and staying up until the parents feel he is tired. I do not feel there should be a set bedtime rule or that the house has to be silent when the baby goes to bed. He will adjust to your schedule if you train him from the beginning.

How often should I feed my baby?

When a newborn comes home from the hospital he may be fed every two to four hours. The infant should be fed on demand - which means feed him when he cries for food. Do not let the infant go more than four hours during the day without a feeding; otherwise, he may get his days and nights mixed up. At night, do not wake the baby to feed him unless he is very small and needs extra weight. In the first three months of life, if the infant wakes up during the night feed him if it has been two hours or more since his last feeding. After three months of age, do not feed him in the middle of the night.

How do I comfort a crying baby?

Lay the baby on his back. Take his legs and put them towards his stomach so he is back in the fetal position. This will generally soothe the baby as it mimics the time he spent in the womb. However, if the baby continues to cry, even after being placed in the fetal position, he is most likely hungry.

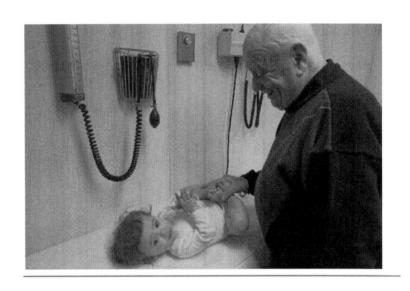

Placing my great-grandson Aaron in the fetal position

CHAPTER 5

PACIFIERS

Should I give my baby a pacifier?

We generally recommend not using a pacifier at all, but certainly not after three months of age as the baby will get addicted to it. The child should learn to pacify himself without using any external device.

After three months of age, the baby will start to move around more which usually results in the pacifier falling to the floor. While a parent may attempt to clean it, if the pacifier is not properly sanitized, germs will go right into the child's mouth.

CHAPTER 6

SLEEP POSITIONS

Should my baby sleep on his back, side or stomach?

Statistics show it is safest for a baby to sleep on his back. Please understand that babies have died of sudden infant death syndrome (SIDS) even in a sitting position in a high chair while being fed. Although you should always place a baby in the crib on his back, once a baby is able to roll onto his stomach on his own (around 5 months of age), it is ok for him to sleep on his stomach if he moves to that position.

What age can I put a stuffed animal or blanket in the crib?

There should be no bumpers, blankets, or stuffed animals in the crib until at least one year of age.

How do I keep my infant warm without a blanket?

When your baby comes home from the hospital, wrap him in a swaddle which acts as a blanket. Your baby should be swaddled only when he sleeps at night or during naps and only in the first few months. *This* also makes the child feel relaxed. When your child starts to get more active (three to four months of age) he should no longer be swaddled to allow him to move around and develop his motor skills. The baby should also be able to comfort himself without getting into the habit of being swaddled. At this point, the baby can transition to a wearable blanket or sleep sack. At one year of age you can begin using a traditional blanket.

CHAPTER 7

SLEEPING

When should my child be sleeping through the night?

We expect the baby to sleep through the night between two and three months of age. That means he should sleep from the time the parents go to sleep (approximately nine to eleven o'clock) until six to nine o'clock in the morning. It is important to try to keep the baby awake between six and nine PM while the parents are up. This should be a child's fussy period. The more the baby fusses in the early evening - the better he is likely to sleep. Later that night, your aim should be to have him go to sleep when you go to sleep. If you allow the baby to take catnaps in the early evening hours, he will likely have trouble falling to sleep later and will be more likely to wake up in the middle of the night. Every baby needs a period of activity. The only real activity he has at two or three months of age is crying. If you pick him up or give him a pacifier every time he cries, you are making a mistake. Do not feel that every time he cries it means something is wrong.

If my baby is crying, how do I make sure he is okay?

CRYING CHECKLIST:

1. Is his diaper dirty?
2. When was the last time I fed him? Could he be hungry?
3. Does he have to burp?
4. Feel him to make sure he is not warm. If he feels warm, take his temperature. Also make sure there is nothing in the sleeping area that is giving him discomfort.

If my baby appears to be okay, should I rock him back to sleep?

If he is not hungry, did not have a dirty diaper, and does not appear to be in any pain or have any fever, do not pick him up to rock him back to sleep or take him into bed with you. Instead, give him a hug and rapidly put him back to bed. Do not feed the baby or put a pacifier in his mouth if the baby is older than three months of age. Generally, formula fed babies sleep through the night sooner than breastfed babies. A bottle fed baby should be sleeping through the night at around two months of age, and a breastfed baby should be sleeping through the night at around three months of age.

What do I do if my child is not sleeping through the night?

If your baby is not sleeping through the night at three months, try feeding him as late as possible right before you go to bed. If a three month old baby starts screaming at two o'clock in the morning, for example, go in every twenty minutes until the baby stops crying to check that everything is okay. The average amount of time the child will cry is ninety minutes. If everything appears to be fine, walk out of the room.

How long will it take to teach my child to sleep through the night?

It generally takes three nights. By the fourth night, he should be sleeping through the night. The first three nights will be torture for parents as they must endure listening to their child crying for long periods of time. Surviving the challenge for three consecutive nights will be rewarded with a fourth night of rest. This is conditioning a new pattern of behavior for your baby.

CHAPTER 8

BREASTFEEDING

Should I breastfeed my baby?

Breastfeeding is likely the healthiest for your baby. Roughly 75 percent of mothers breastfeed. I suggest that mothers do what they prefer or what is most comfortable for them. Breastfeeding will only work well if the mother has a desire to do so. If the mother is only doing it because she is told she has to do it or feels pressured, chances are it will not work well and both the mother and the child will be unhappy.

How long should my baby breastfeed per feeding?

The mother should breastfeed about twenty minutes each feeding. Realize that ninety percent of the milk the baby gets with breastfeeding is in the first five minutes. The rest of the time, the baby is primarily using the mother as a pacifier. The baby should be burped every five minutes. If you are breastfeeding, check with your doctor before taking any medications because they will affect the breast milk.

Is it okay for mothers to consume alcohol while breastfeeding?

In our practice, we suggest that the mother abstain from alcohol until the baby is at least three months of age. After three months, if a mother wants to have an occasional drink, wait at least two hours before breastfeeding.

Chapter 9

FORMULA FEEDING

What formula would you recommend using?

A variety of brands exist that mimic breast milk. While there may not be much difference in each brand's ingredients, some babies seem to prefer one over another. So if your infant doesn't take well to one brand, transition to another.

There are sophisticated formulas for a colicky baby who does not do well on regular formula. A colicky baby is one that has severe abdominal pain which causes the baby to be cranky. There are also formulas such as soybean or goat's milk formulas which are used in specific cases if the baby cannot tolerate other formulas.

How much milk should my baby drink?

A newborn usually takes one to two ounces of formula per feeding and should be burped every ounce. Slowly increase the formula by half an ounce at a time. The baby should work his way up to six ounces, which usually takes anywhere from four to six weeks. At this point, he should be burped every two ounces.

CHAPTER 10

SPITTING UP/VOMITTING

Why do I need to burp my baby?

Babies need to burp to minimize colic, gas and projectile vomiting.

How do I get my infant to burp?

- Sitting the baby in an upright position and gently rubbing his back
- Laying him flat on your lap for a few seconds and then proceeding to put him in a sitting position again

- Placing him on your chest or shoulder (where his head is above your shoulder) and patting his back

The baby will likely start fidgeting or bringing his legs towards his stomach indicating that he needs to burp. Please note sometimes it can take as long as 10 to 15 minutes to get the baby to burp.

How do I get my child to stop spitting up?

Many babies vomit after feeding as a result of reflux, which occurs when the milk comes back up from the stomach into the esophagus tube. These babies gain weight even though they spit up. To reduce reflux, put your baby in a sitting position (or a 45 degree angle) after feeding rather than laying him flat. This will allow the feeding to go into his stomach faster and stay there rather than coming back up. You may also want to speak to your pediatrician about one of many medicines available to help feedings stay down.

What age should the spitting up stop?

Spitting up can persist until about nine months of age when the valve develops between the esophagus and stomach which helps the baby keep food down.

Should I be concerned if my baby vomits forcefully?

If a child has sudden or vigorous (projectile) vomiting you have to be concerned about pyloric stenosis where the outlet of the stomach is constricted. This requires a very simple procedure to release the obstruction at the end of the stomach. Seen mostly in male babies, pyloric stenosis is usually diagnosed at around three to five weeks of age. Just because a baby vomits after feeding does not mean that the child has this condition.

CHAPTER 11

DIAPER RASH

AND DRY SKIN

Any tips on preventing diaper rash?

You can avoid a diaper rash by changing his diaper more often and making sure his bottom is clean. If he does get a diaper rash, use Desitin, A&D ointment or Triple Paste to try to remedy the rash. If he does not respond to the ointments, contact a physician for further diagnosis.

What can I do if my baby's skin is dry?

If he has dry skin, we recommend using moisturizing lotion such as Eucerin or Aquaphor. Consult your physician if the child has extremely dry skin that does not respond to the moisturizers. Extreme dry skin may be due to a condition called eczema.

CHAPTER 12

DEVELOPMENTAL STAGES

At what age should my child hear, see, smile, laugh, sit, turnover, reach for objects, crawl, walk and talk?

AVERAGE AGE OF DEVELOPMENT
FIRST YEAR OF LIFE

newborn	• hears • sees
2-3 months	• follows objects with his eyes • smiles
5 months	• reaches for objects • turns over

6 months	• **laughs** • **babbles**
8 months	• **sits up**
9 months	• **crawls**
12 months	• **walks** • **talks**

When the baby is born he should be able to hear and see. He starts to visually follow objects at about two months of age. At two to three months of age, you should see his first social smile, and at about six months, the baby should start laughing.

You will see smiles before that, but usually not in response to any social situation. He should start reaching for objects and turning over by himself at about five months of age. At around six to eight months of age, he should start babbling. He should be sitting at about eight months of age and crawling at about nine months of age. Walking should begin around one year of age. A child will start using words around the same time he starts walking (12 months).

Babies develop at different rates of speed, and a baby sitting at six months of age may not be crawling until eleven months of age. This doesn't mean that something is wrong.

What is the average weight and height gain in the first two years of life?

The baby should gain about one to one and one-half pounds each month for the first year of life. The average child grows around one inch each month until age one.

During the second year of life, the baby should grow four to six inches on average.

Is it normal to feel soft spots on my baby's head?

When your baby is born, the bones of the head are not yet joined together. There will be two small indentations - one in the front of the head which is called the anterior fontanelle and a small indentation in the back of the head which is called the posterior fontanelle. The indentation in the back of the head closes at about eight weeks; the one on the front of the head does not close until approximately eighteen months.

CHAPTER 13

IMMUNIZATIONS

Are vaccines safe?

Some parents question whether their child should get immunizations because they have heard they may be dangerous. It has been proven over the years that immunizations are far less dangerous than the risks of not being immunized.

The infant's immunity in the first ninety days of life is protected by the mother. For example, if the mother has had the measles shot or the disease, the baby is protected from the measles.

Measles is a disease that can affect children for the rest of their lives. Measles is no longer the threat it once was, thanks to the availability of immunizations.

In the early twentieth century, there was a problem with children getting polio, a disease that permanently paralyzes limbs and/or other muscles of many children. Breathing was sometimes compromised by this horrible disease, which ultimately lead to many deaths. Thankfully, today immunizations now protect against polio.

Years ago, there was such an effective immunization against small pox that this disease has been totally eradicated and children no longer need the smallpox immunization.

Many physicians and clinics will give several immunizations at once. In our practice, we try never to give more than two immunizations at a time unless the child is far behind and needs them to get into school.

CHART OF IMMUNIZATIONS

newborn	Vitamin K Hepatitis B – 1 of 3
1 month	Hepatitis B - 2 of 3
2 months	DPT (Diphtheria, Whooping cough and Tetanus) - 1 of 5 Polio - 1 of 4
3 months	Hib (Haemophilus influenza type b) - 1 of 4 Prevnar (Pneumococcal) - 1 of 4
4 months	DPT - 2 of 5 Polio - 2 of 4
5 months	Hib - 2 of 4 Prevnar - 2 of 4
6 months	DPT - 3 of 5
7 months	Prevnar - 3 of 4 Influenza (flu) - 1/2 dose

8 months	**Hib - 3 of 4 Influenza (flu) - 1/2 dose**
12 months	**Hemoglobin Hepatitis B - 3 of 3**
15 months	**MMR (measles, mumps, rubella) - 1 of 2**
18 months	**DPT - 4 of 5 Polio - 3 of 4**
21 months	**Prevnar - 4 of 4 Hib - 4 of 4**
24 months	**Chickenpox (Varicella) - 1 of 2**

There are no other vaccines given until kindergarten age when the child will get boosters.

5 YEAR OLD BOOSTERS

MMR

2 of 2

DPT

5 of 5

Polio

4 of 4

Chickenpox

2 of 2

Some physicians also give the hepatitis A and three doses of Rotavirus vaccines which are optional and are not required to enter school.

We recommend giving your baby the influenza (flu) vaccine after six months of age. In our practice, the first time a child receives the flu vaccine, if he is under the age of three, he should receive one-half dose followed by another one-half dose a month later. Thereafter, a child under the age of three should receive a single one-half dose annually. Once the child is over the age of three, full dosages may be administered each year.

CHAPTER 14

TRANSITIONING TO SOLIDS

What should I do if my baby refuses to eat?

Never force a child to eat; the child will eat when he gets hungry.

At what age should I start my baby on solid foods?

Before six months of age, medically most babies need nothing but milk. Some babies require solid foods earlier than six months of age because they are not being satisfied by just milk. If the baby consistently drinks six ounces of milk at a feeding and if he is not sleeping through the night, he is likely waking up because he is hungry. At this time, we would allow the baby to start solid foods.

What age does food become more important than milk?

After six months of age, food is much more important than milk. Milk is not a significant source of iron and if the baby were to exist on milk alone after six months of age, the baby would be anemic from a lack of iron.

What should be the first solid food?

The baby's first solid food should be rice cereal twice a day, given at breakfast and dinner. Rice cereal comes as a dry powdered cereal. It doesn't make a difference what brand you use. Start off with a teaspoon and work up to two tablespoons of rice cereal mixed with enough of the baby's formula to make the consistency like mashed potatoes. Even after starting the rice cereal, always begin the baby's feeding with his formula or breast milk when he is ravenously hungry (such as after a night's sleep). After feeding him the milk, burp him, offer him the solid food, and then give him the rest of the bottle.

After your child has been on rice cereal for a month, introduce stage 1 strained fruits (puréed fruit with no pulp), starting with a teaspoon and working up to two tablespoons per meal.

Three or four weeks later, begin feeding the baby strained vegetables which should be given at lunch and dinner.

I recommend that the baby be fed solid foods from a spoon rather than a pouch so he begins to experience how to properly use utensils.

The following month, start the baby on strained meats and vegetables. If he doesn't seem to like meats, try combining the meats with vegetables. You can purée your own meats, vegetables and fruits as long as it is fine in consistency. As the baby gets older and more teeth develop, gradually work up to stage 2 foods and eventually stage 3.

FOOD CHART

MEALS	AROUND 6 MONTHS	1 MONTH LATER	1 MONTH LATER	1 MONTH LATER
BREAKFAST	milk rice cereal	milk rice cereal strained fruit	milk rice cereal strained fruit	milk rice cereal strained fruit
LUNCH	milk	milk strained fruit	milk strained vegetable strained fruit	milk strained vegetable and meat or combination of both strained fruit
SNACK	milk	milk	milk	milk
DINNER	milk rice cereal	milk rice cereal strained fruit	milk strained vegetable or rice cereal strained fruit	milk strained vegetable and meat or combination of both strained fruit
BEDTIME	milk	milk	milk	milk

How do I know if my child is allergic to certain foods?

Stay on one food for at least three days before moving on to another. If your child does not break out in a rash or have any allergic reaction, on the fourth day you may try another food. Repeat this for any new fruit, vegetable or meat.

When should I stop breastfeeding/ bottle feeding my baby?

At one year of age the baby should be weaned off the breast/bottle as both are bad for the child's developing teeth. The child should use a regular cup or sippy cup until two years of age.

Any tips on how to get a baby off the breast/bottle and drinking from a cup?

At nine months of age start taking away one breast/bottle feeding and substituting a sippy cup or regular cup instead. Take one more breast/bottle feeding away each month.

AGE	BOTTLES	SIPPY CUPS
9 months	3	1
10 months	2	2
11 months	1	3
12 months	0	4

For example, at ten months of age, the baby should get two feedings from the breast/bottle and two sippy or regular cups each day. At eleven months of age, he should get one feeding from the breast/bottle and three sippy or regular cups a day. By twelve months of age, the baby should be off of all breast/bottles and using only a sippy or regular cup. Expect your

59

baby to drink less fluid from a sippy cup than from a bottle.

What age do I start to give whole milk?

We recommend using whole cow's milk beginning at one year of age. The four percent fat in regular vitamin D homogenized whole milk is helpful for brain development. We do not recommend low-fat milk to be used in the first two years of life.

CHAPTER 15

CONSTIPATION/DIARRHEA

What if my infant has not had a bowel movement in a couple of days?

It is normal for the child to have anywhere from one to six bowel movements each day; however, some babies will go once every two days. If the baby is not uncomfortable, nothing should be done. If, however, he seems uncomfortable and cranky, take the tip of an infant glycerin suppository and insert it into the rectum about a quarter of an inch (not too far) and make a round circle like the hands of a clock. It's very rare that you have to give medication to a baby who is constipated. Adding one tablespoon of Karo syrup to four to six ounces of formula will help him move his bowels easier. If the baby is being breastfed, the mother can increase the fruits in her diet to help loosen his stools.

When starting the baby on solid foods, fruits will help loosen his stool while cereal will make him more constipated.

What should I do if my infant has diarrhea?

If the infant is having very watery stools five to seven times a day, take him off milk and give him a rehydrating solution, such as Pedialyte, for twenty-four hours. Then progress from Pedialyte to half strength formula (half Pedialyte, half formula). When his bowels are normal for 24 hours, he may then progress to full strength formula.

If the infant is being breastfed, continue breastfeeding, however, the mother should not eat any fruits or juices in her diet for at least a week.

If the child is already on solid foods, eliminate all fruits and juices from his diet for several days.

CHAPTER 16

TEETH

When will teeth appear?

While most babies get their first teeth around six months of age, it varies on a case by case basis. It is not unusual for one child to develop their first tooth at four months of age and another child to get their first tooth at one year of age. The first teeth to emerge are usually the lower front teeth, which are the biting teeth (not the chewing teeth). A good formula to use on approximately how many teeth your child should have is taking the baby's age in months and subtracting six. For example, a twelve months old child will have approximately six teeth.

How should I take care of my child's teeth?

As soon as a baby's first tooth appears, the parent should begin to brush morning and night with a small toothbrush or silicone bristle finger toothbrush and rice sized amount of fluoridated baby's toothpaste. If the baby does not like the texture of the toothpaste, stick the toothbrush into a non-alcohol based fluoride dental rinse instead (such as ACT for kids). If the baby does not tolerate the toothbrush, gently rub his teeth and gums with tooth wipes (such as Spiffies or Xylitol wipes).

What happens if my baby is on a bottle/breast more than one year?

The child is much more likely to develop cavities if he has been breastfed or drinking from a bottle for more than a year.

If my child sucks his thumb/fingers, how does this affect his developing teeth?

Thumb/finger sucking is difficult to stop and often leads to protruding or "buck" teeth.

How can I get my baby out of the habit of sucking his thumb/fingers?

At around one year of age the best solution is to put a small glove or sock over the child's hand before bedtime to prevent him from putting his thumb/fingers into his mouth.

CHAPTER 17

FEVER

What is considered a fever and how should it be treated?

A fever is a temperature over 100 degrees. If the temperature is under 101, we would not recommend any treatment for relieving the fever. If the temperature is 101-103, we suggest taking infant Tylenol drops using the dosage on the box. If the temperature is 103 or higher, we advise giving ibuprofen, such as infant Motrin or Advil, along with sponge bathing the child with lukewarm water. If the temperature remains over 102 even though you are using Advil or Motrin, we recommend rotating every three hours between ibuprofen and Tylenol. That way the baby will be getting a different medicine every three hours even though each individual medicine is given six hours apart.

Always alert your physician if your baby's temperature is above 101 so the child can be examined for possible secondary infections. Ninety percent of infections in children are viral infections which do not respond to antibiotics. If a child has a sore throat and fever, a throat culture should be taken to make sure he does not have a strep throat. "Strep" is a germ called Streptococcus which can cause complications such as rheumatic fever if it is not treated with antibiotic within ten days. Your doctor can do a rapid culture in 10 minutes, or a more accurate 24 hour culture, to determine if the child will need an antibiotic. A strep throat is very rare in a child under the age of two.

Antibiotics will not cure common colds but may cure bacterial infections (which rarely occur in children).

How long will a fever last with a viral infection?

Generally, a fever will last up to three to four days with a viral infection. A cough, however, will probably last two weeks or more.

What should I have in the house in case my baby gets sick?

Every parent should be equipped with a cold air humidifier/vaporizer. Since you cannot give medications for congestion and coughing to a child under three years of age, the humidifier will help alleviate these symptoms.

Also keep Pedialyte, an ear or rectal thermometer, baby Tylenol, and infant Advil or Motrin in your home.

When can my child return to daycare after he is ill?

Once the temperature stays below 100 degrees for 24 hours without medication, the child can return to daycare.

CHAPTER 18

POTTY TRAINING

When should I start potty training?

Girls are easier to potty train than boys. The average girl potty trains between ages two and three. The average boy potty trains between two and one-half and three and one- half years of age. The harder you try to potty train, the harder it will be. If your child thinks the biggest thing in the world to you is to have him get potty trained, the later he will likely be trained. The more the child sees you do, the more he will want to copy. For this reason, do not ask every day if he wants to go to the bathroom. Let him observe you and ask "Do you want to copy me?" Chances are he will.

The more patience you have with him, the earlier he will be potty trained. Punishment will get you nowhere, however, if you reward him it will certainly help. Some children take up to four or five years to be potty trained.

CHAPTER 19

JEALOUSY-ANOTHER SIBLING

Will my child be jealous when I have another child?

The age of your child will determine how jealous he will become when a sibling arrives.

If the child is under two years of age when the infant is born, he will likely not be jealous. If your child is between two and four years of age he will realize things are different. For example, when you put a baby into his crib, the older child might get jealous because he thinks the baby is taking over his space. This is why we advise trying to get the older child sleeping in a bed before his new sibling arrives. If a child is older than four years of age, chances are there will be less jealousy issues when the baby is born.

CHAPTER 20

WRAP-UP

Parents should spend as much time as possible with their babies. The growing developmental years go extremely fast, and you don't want to miss these milestones as babies learn to smile, reach, sit, walk and talk.

DO	DON'T
Take pre-natal vitamins with folic acid three months prior to trying to conceive	Take any medications without medical advice while pregnant or breastfeeding
Be as calm as possible during pregnancy and as a parent	Consume any alcohol or tobacco during pregnancy
Keep your baby on your schedule – start from the beginning	Rock the baby as a routine to get him to sleep
Immunize your child to prevent him from getting dangerous diseases	Use a pacifier after three months of age
Strive to have your baby sleeping through the night by three months of age	
Wean your baby off the bottle/breast by one year of age	
Have fun, love and enjoy your family	

About the Author

Stanley Stein, MD

Dr. Stanley Stein has been a pediatrician since 1962. He has seen over 50,000 patients and given over one million vaccines.

He was raised in Brooklyn, New York; his father was a dentist and his mother was a biology major. He is the oldest of three children - all of whom became doctors.

Dr. Stein earned his bachelor's degree in Psychology from the University of Vermont. He was a Dean's list student and president of the senior men's honorary society. In addition to being in the top ten percent of his class in academics, he was active in many extracurricular activities. He served as director of University of Vermont's winter carnival, president of his fraternity Tau Epsilon Phi, and president of the University of Vermont inter-fraternity council.

After obtaining his undergraduate degree in 1955, he received his medical degree from University of Vermont in 1959. From there, he went on to New York Bellevue Hospital for his pediatric internship followed by a rotation at Baby's Hospital, a part of Columbia Presbyterian Medical Center, where he completed his residency in pediatrics. Dr. Stein then served his coast guard obligation where he established the pediatric ward on the undergraduate campus of John Hopkins University at the U.S. Public Health Hospital. In 1964, he went into private practice in Pennsylvania. Three years later, he became Chief of Pediatrics at St. Luke's Hospital in Bethlehem, Pennsylvania - a position he held for 32 years.

In 2018, Dr. Stanley Stein celebrated his 55th year of private practice.

Index

A special thanks to Buddy Lesavoy, Haley Zimring, Jayne Diehl, and Dana Zale Gerard

Made in the USA
Middletown, DE
20 November 2018